DK SUPER History

BOSTON TEA PARTY

Discover what happened at Boston Harbor in 1773 and why the events of the day became a symbol of colonial resistance

PRODUCED FOR DK BY
Editorial Just Content Limited
Design Studio Noel

Author Marissa Moss

Senior Editor Ankita Awasthi Tröger
Editor Hattie Hansford
Senior Art Editor Gilda Pacitti
Graphic Story Illustrator Matt Garbutt
Managing Editor Carine Tracanelli
Managing Art Editor Sarah Corcoran
Pre-Production Coordinator Shanker Prasad
Pre-Production Designer Jaypal Chauhan
Production Controller Rebecca Parton
Publisher Sarah Forbes
Managing Director, Learning Hilary Fine

First published in Great Britain in 2025 by
Dorling Kindersley Limited
20 Vauxhall Bridge Road,
London SW1V 2SA

The authorised representative in the EEA is
Dorling Kindersley Verlag GmbH. Arnulfstr. 124,
80636 Munich, Germany

10 9 8 7 6 5 4 3 2 1
001–350112–Sep/2025

A CIP catalogue record for this book
is available from the British Library.
ISBN: 978-0-2417-4471-0

Printed and bound in China

www.dk.com

This book was made with Forest Stewardship Council™ certified paper – one small step in DK's commitment to a sustainable future.
Learn more at www.dk.com/uk/information/sustainability

Contents

History in Perspective 4
Key Events: What Happened When 6
Key People: Who's Who 8
Key Location: Boston Harbor 10
The British Empire 12
The Importance of Tea 14
The American Colonies 16
The Cost of War 18
No Vote, No Tax! 20
The Tea Act 22
Plans and Protests 24
Tea Overboard! 26
Trouble Brewing 28
Not Tolerable! 32
The Road to Revolution 34
Lessons from History 36
Uncovering the Truth: Primary Sources 38
Uncovering the Truth: Secondary Sources 40
Vocabulary Builder: A Night I Will Never Forget 42
Glossary 44
Index 46

Words in **bold** are explained in the glossary on page 44.

History in Perspective

On a December night in 1773, a group of American **colonists** took dramatic action against the British **government**. The group was called the Sons of Liberty. First, they put on disguises. Then, they boarded British ships **docked** in Boston Harbor. Finally, they dumped 342 chests of tea into the water. Tea was worth a lot of money at the time. The British government **taxed** it at a high rate. This event would later be known as the Boston Tea Party. It was a protest against unfair taxation and the way Britain was ruling its **colonies**. The American colonists were unhappy that they had to pay taxes with no **representation** in **parliament**.

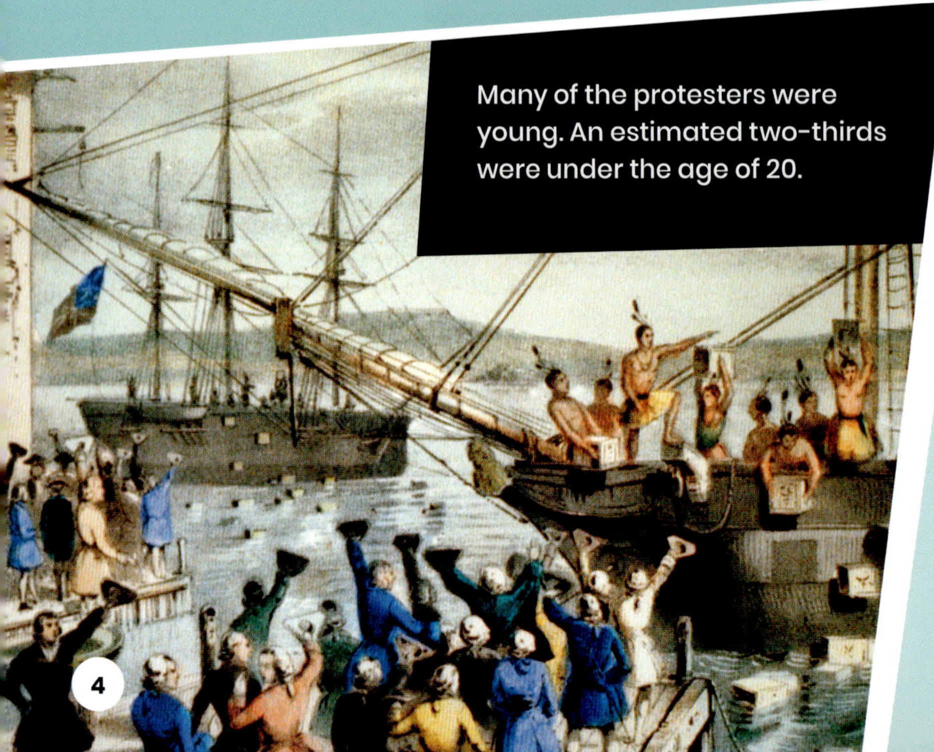

Many of the protesters were young. An estimated two-thirds were under the age of 20.

Where and when?

The Boston Tea Party happened at a place called Griffin's Wharf in Boston Harbor, Massachusetts, on 16 December 1773.

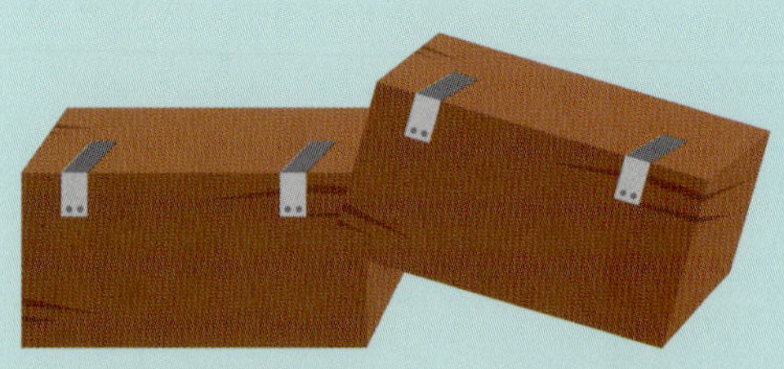

The Sons of Liberty destroyed British cargo. This showed how strongly they felt about their rights. Their actions captured the mood of many colonists at the time. It was a sign of much bigger changes to come.

Think about it

What kinds of **sources** could we use to learn about the Boston Tea Party?

Who was involved?

The Boston Tea Party was planned by the Sons of Liberty, a group made up of colonists who were unhappy with British rule. Most of its members were men from English families living in or around Boston. There were also colonists with Irish, Scottish, Portuguese, French and African backgrounds. The lead-up to the event involved British people and companies too, such as the royal governor of the British North American Province of Massachusetts Bay, the British prime minister, and the British East India Company, which owned all the tea that was thrown into the harbour.

Different perspectives

Different groups in society may have deeply contrasting experiences of events. Official records of the past often only present one side of the story. This means that they can't reflect the experiences of everyone affected. To understand what happened, it is important that we look at events from more than one point of view.

Key Events
WHAT HAPPENED WHEN

The Boston Tea Party changed the relationship between the American colonies and **Great Britain** forever. Here are some of the key events that led up to the event.

1763

10 FEBRUARY

The Seven Years' War between Great Britain and France ends. Britain gains more land in North America, including Canada. France loses a lot of its **territories** in North America, the Caribbean and India.

1765

MARCH–NOVEMBER

The war leaves Great Britain in a lot of **debt**. The British Parliament passes the Stamp Act to raise money, requiring American colonies to pay tax on printed materials. This leads to protests throughout the colonies and **boycotts** of British products.

1767

29 JUNE AND 2 JULY

The British government passes the Townshend Acts. These acts make it legal to add tax to **imported** goods such as glass, paint, paper, lead and tea.

1770

5 MARCH

British soldiers shoot at a crowd of hundreds of American colonists. They kill five people. This is referred to as the Boston Massacre.

APRIL

There is more unrest in the colonies and more British products are boycotted. The British Parliament finally **repeals** all the Townshend taxes, except for the tea tax.

1773

NOVEMBER

The Sons of Liberty meet secretly in Boston to plan a protest. They want to destroy the tea that is on British ships docked in Boston Harbor.

16 DECEMBER

The Sons of Liberty carry out their plan. They throw 342 chests of tea from British ships into the sea. This is later known as the Boston Tea Party.

1774

31 MARCH

The first of the Intolerable Acts is passed, which closes Boston Harbor. Other Intolerable Acts follow soon after.

Key People
WHO'S WHO

The Boston Tea Party changed the course of American history. American colonists acted to show they were unhappy with British rule. They were also frustrated that they had no representation in parliament. They were determined to achieve change. In Great Britain, leaders were also determined to keep the American colonies under their control. Here are some of the key people in this story.

American colonists

Samuel Adams

Crispus Attucks

A formerly enslaved man. He was shot and killed by British soldiers during the Boston Massacre of 1770.

Samuel Adams

A tax collector who became a Boston politician. He was one of the leaders of the Sons of Liberty and campaigned for colonial rights.

John Hancock

A **merchant** and politician in Boston. Hancock is known for his large signature on the American **Declaration of Independence**.

Paul Revere

A silversmith, engraver and active member of the Sons of Liberty. He often acted as a messenger in important events leading up to the American Revolution.

British leaders

King George III

The king of Great Britain from 1760 to 1820 and of Ireland from 1801 to 1820. He used war to expand the British **Empire**, especially against France. He was determined to keep control of the American colonies.

Lord Frederick North

The prime minister of Great Britain from 1770 to 1782. He wanted to make sure the American colonies stayed loyal to the British **Crown**.

Thomas Hutchinson

The royal governor of the Province of Massachusetts Bay from 1771 to 1774. He was a merchant who was loyal to Great Britain. He did not want the tea to be thrown into the sea.

Charles Townshend

The **chancellor of the exchequer**, in charge of Great Britain's money. He came up with the Townshend Acts.

King George III

Thomas Hutchinson

Key Location
BOSTON HARBOR

In the 1770s, life in Boston Harbor was very busy. At the time, the harbour was one of the most important ports in North America. Boston's ships traded with other colonies and were part of bigger trading routes that crossed the Atlantic Ocean. It was the main port for ships bringing goods from Great Britain, such as textiles, ship supplies and tea. Products from the colonies, including wood, fish and rum, were sent from Boston Harbor to Great Britain. By the late 1700s, some ships from Boston sailed as far as Shanghai, in China. The harbour was also used by the British to send people, soldiers and supplies to the American colonies.

By 1770, the population of Boston was around 16,000. Many people had jobs that related to the harbour. They built ships, made ropes and went fishing. The harbour helped Boston grow and become an important city.

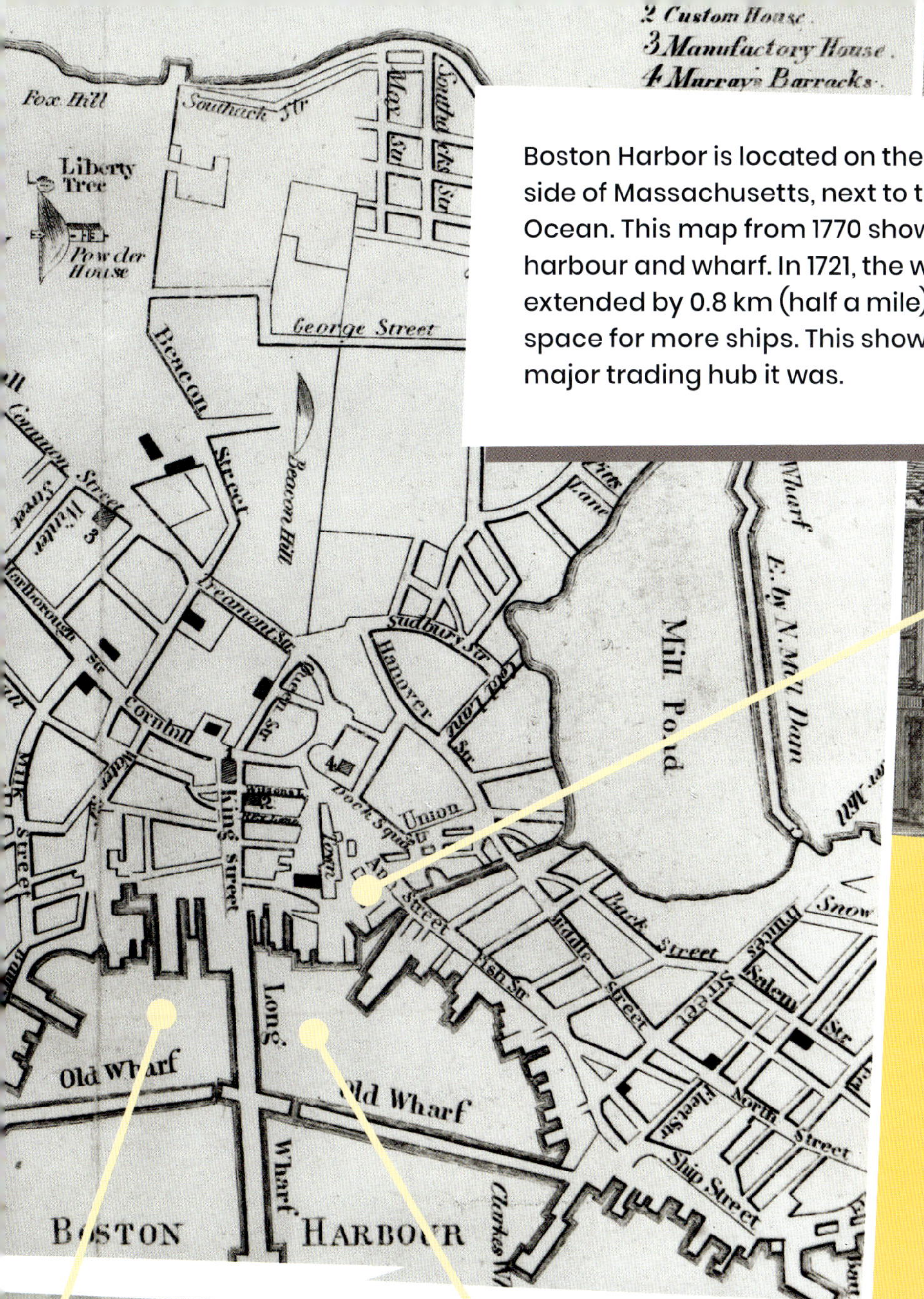

Boston Harbor is located on the eastern side of Massachusetts, next to the Atlantic Ocean. This map from 1770 shows the harbour and wharf. In 1721, the wharf was extended by 0.8 km (half a mile) to allow space for more ships. This shows what a major trading hub it was.

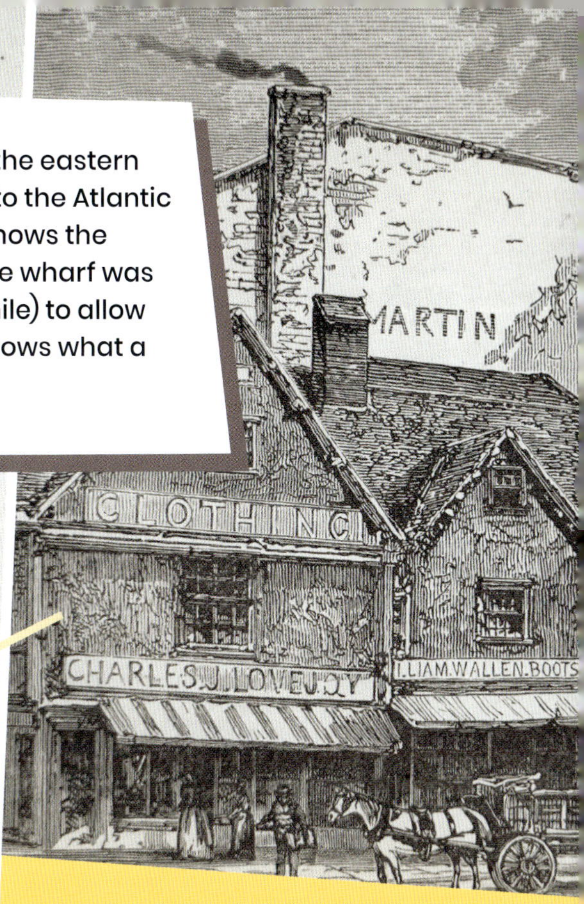

This picture of the Old Feather Store building is from the 19th century. When the store was built in 1680, it was right next to the water. The waves from the sea would come up to its doors. It is thought the Sons of Liberty met here to plan the Boston Tea Party.

Today, the harbour is called the Port of Boston. It is still used for trade, but its role has changed over the years. Ships still deliver goods from other countries, especially cars. There are also a lot of cruise ships that carry tourists who want to visit the city. The port is an important place for catching and selling fish.

The British Empire

In the late 1700s, Great Britain was one of the most powerful nations in the world, with a large and far-reaching empire. Great Britain ruled over millions of people in countries across Africa, Asia, North America, South America, Australia and the Caribbean.

This map shows some of Great Britain's American colonies in 1763. The colouring was added later and may not be completely accurate, but the British-controlled territories are mostly shown in pink or green.

Think about it

Sources may be changed after they were originally created so it is always important to look at them carefully. Can you think of reasons why the colouring on this map might not reflect what we would expect to see?

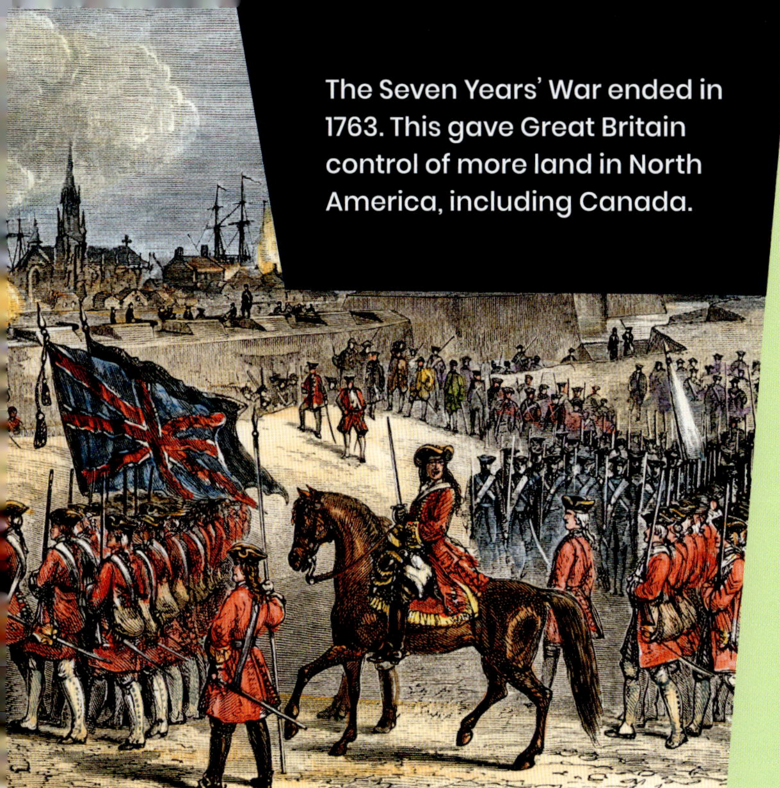

The Seven Years' War ended in 1763. This gave Great Britain control of more land in North America, including Canada.

A GLOBAL POWER

Great Britain fought and won many wars against other powerful countries in Europe, like France and Spain. Britain had a strong army and a dominant navy (with over 600 ships and 120,000 men in 1799), which helped it win battles on land and at sea. The navy protected British ships and **trade routes**, while the army fought in many conflicts, including the Seven Years' War. Because of these victories, Britain gained more land around the world, making its empire even bigger and more powerful.

COLONIAL FORCE

The British government sent settlers to build new colonies in places such as Australia, India and the Caribbean. British settlers forcibly took land away from **Indigenous** communities, claiming it as their own. They also enslaved millions of Indigenous peoples, with Indigenous communities facing many years of violence. Millions suffered and died due to Great Britain's expansion.

In 1770, Great Britain began to take control of Australia. They forced First Australians off their land. It is estimated that at least 20,000 were killed because of colonial violence.

By the late 1700s, the British Royal Navy was the most powerful in the world.

ECONOMIC STRENGTH

The British Empire gained more and more land. This gave them even more valuable items to trade, such as tea from China and spices from India. The British also profited from enslavement. For example, enslaved people in the Caribbean were forced to work without pay on sugar plantations. Sugar was a very valuable **commodity**, and the British sold it around the world. These actions helped make Great Britain rich, and gave it the money to build an even stronger military.

The Importance of Tea

It might seem strange to think of tea as a valuable commodity. Today, it is widely available to most people. But this was not the case in the past. In 1600, Dutch traders first introduced tea to the American colonies. Around 1650, they introduced it to Great Britain. However, high taxes meant that tea cost a lot to import from China. This made it an expensive luxury that only the rich could afford.

Fascinating fact

In 1657, Thomas Garway became the first person to sell tea in Great Britain. He owne a coffee house in London. He even made a pamphlet to explain what tea was.

Tea was a popular drink with **aristocrats**. They would often share it with guests to show off their wealth.

THE EAST INDIA COMPANY

Queen Elizabeth I, queen of England and Ireland, set up the East India Company in 1600. It was formed to trade valuable items. These included things like spices, tea and silk from South Asia and Southeast Asia. The company played an important role in moving tea around the world. It was also the only company allowed to import tea into Great Britain. The East India Company set the price and managed the tea supply at home and in the colonies.

Trading tea earned the East India Company a lot of money. It was very powerful. It was based in London and operated until 1874.

TEA'S POPULARITY GROWS

As tea grew in popularity, demand for it **skyrocketed**. But most people could not afford to buy it legally. **Smugglers seized** the opportunity. They started bringing tea into Great Britain and the American colonies on small boats. Some estimates suggest that smugglers brought in more than 7,500 metric tons (8,000 tons) of tea into Great Britain in the late 1700s. In 1760, around 450 metric tons (500 tons) of tea came into the American colonies. Three-quarters of it was smuggled.

Smugglers risked their lives to bring tea into Britain and the American colonies. It was dangerous work, but the rewards were high.

This is the East India Company's **coat of arms**. The trade it carried out was so important to Great Britain that in 1757 it was given its own army to help it control British territories in India.

The American Colonies

When they first arrived in the early 1600s, European settlers found colonial America an exciting place to be. People there had a chance to start new lives in a new place. Many colonists worked hard to build homes and businesses. They also traded products such as tobacco, wheat, corn and weapons with other colonies and countries. As more and more new settlers arrived, the colonists developed their own ways of socializing, working, dressing and speaking.

This painting shows colonists arriving at Jamestown, Virginia.

TRADING IN THE COLONIES

The trading undertaken by American colonists helped settlers' communities grow and become wealthier. They even traded some products with Great Britain, including ships, furs and iron.

Indigenous communities traded furs, animal skins and native crops with settlers for European goods such as metal tools, weapons, cloth and glass beads.

THE BOSTON MASSACRE

American colonists continued to develop their culture, communities and economy. Nonetheless, they remained a part of Britain's empire and were governed by the British Parliament in London. Many of the colonists believed that this was unfair. They wanted to have greater control over their land. In March 1770, these tensions boiled over in Boston. Hundreds of American colonists confronted a small group of British soldiers. The British soldiers fired their guns into the crowd. They killed five colonists, including Crispus Attucks, a formerly enslaved man.

Crispus Attucks was shot and killed by British soldiers during the Boston Massacre. He was later known as "the brave soldier of the Revolutionary War".

Paul Revere, one of the Sons of Liberty, was a talented engraver and silversmith and also created several notable political cartoons. In March 1770, he printed and sold this story about the massacre. It included his engraving of the event, copied from an engraving by Boston artist Henry Pelham .

The Cost of War

George Grenville

Great Britain had won the Seven Years' War – but war was expensive. Britain's debt had doubled from £75 million in 1756 to £133 million in 1763. Paying just the **interest** on this debt used up half of the country's national budget each year. The government, led by Prime Minister George Grenville, was under a lot of pressure to find a solution. So, it came up with a plan – it decided to raise money by taxing American colonists.

THE STAMP ACT

The Stamp Act of 1765 was a law passed by the British government. It required American colonists to pay a tax on printed materials such as newspapers, legal documents, playing cards and pamphlets. These printed materials had to be made on special paper with a stamp showing the tax was paid.

The colonists were furious about the new tax. They organised protests and decided to boycott British products. Just four months later, the government had no choice but to repeal the Stamp Act.

THE TOWNSHEND ACTS

In 1767, the government of Great Britain passed the Townshend Acts, which introduced new taxes on various products, including paper, glass, paint, lead and tea. The colonists reacted with anger. Groups like the Sons of Liberty were formed to help protest against these taxes. Most of the Townshend Acts were repealed in 1770, but the damage had been done. Significantly, the tax on tea remained.

The acts were named after Charles Townshend, the chancellor of the exchequer. He came up with the idea to tax goods used by the American colonists.

The Treaty of Paris was signed in 1763. This ended the Seven Years' War. But Great Britain's victory over France had come at a huge cost.

Think about it

What impact would these taxes have had on the everyday lives of American colonists?

No Vote, No Tax!

American colonists were outraged by the Boston Massacre, Stamp Act and Townshend Acts. Their relationship with the British government was worse than ever. The colonists did not want to pay expensive taxes. And they had no representation in parliament. This meant they had no say in decisions that affected them.

The British Parliament made decisions that affected the American colonies.

This sketch shows American colonists complaining about the Stamp Act.

NO REPRESENTATION

The phrase "no taxation without representation" became a powerful **motto**. It meant it was unfair to pay taxes while having no say in decisions that affected you.

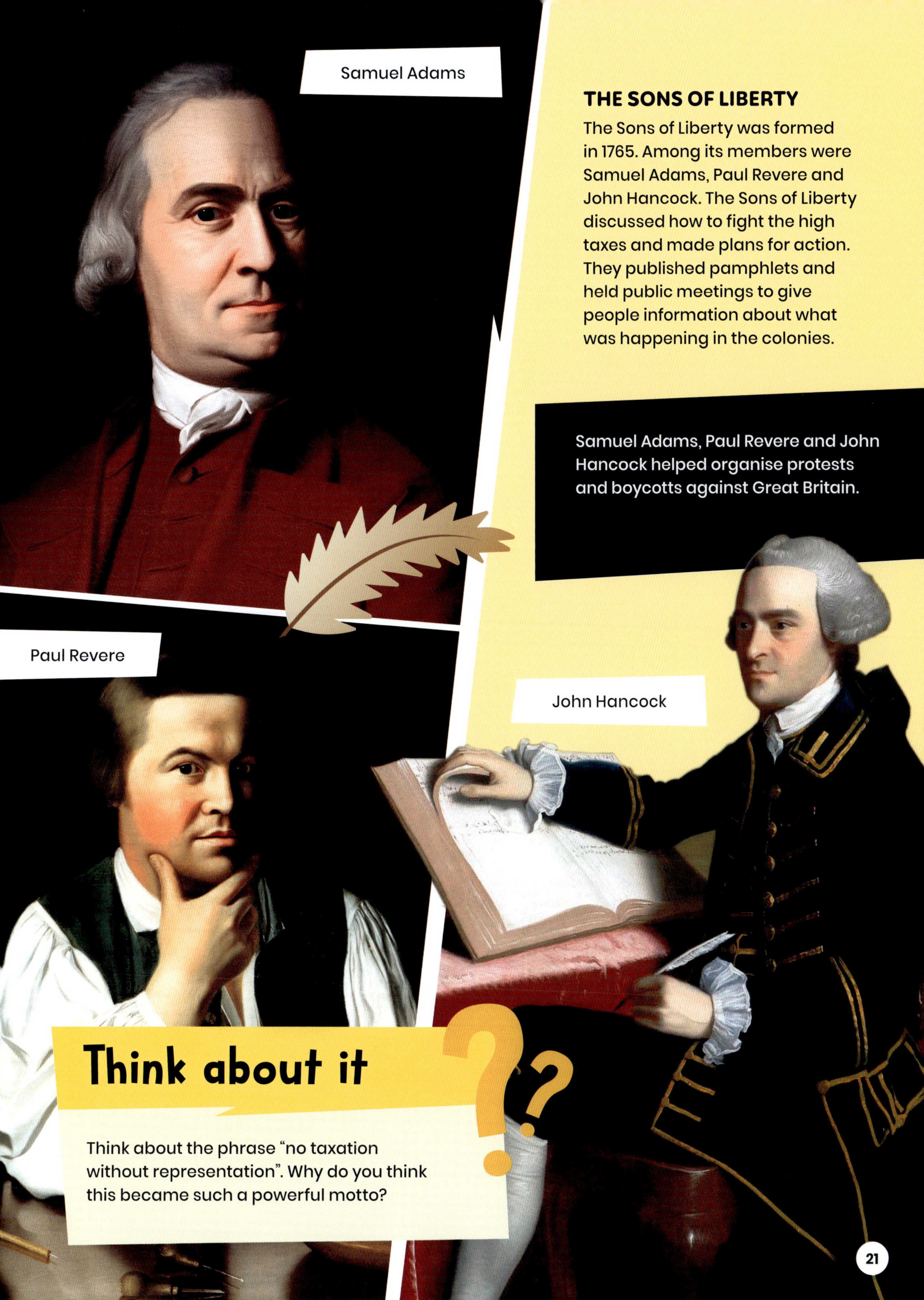

THE SONS OF LIBERTY

The Sons of Liberty was formed in 1765. Among its members were Samuel Adams, Paul Revere and John Hancock. The Sons of Liberty discussed how to fight the high taxes and made plans for action. They published pamphlets and held public meetings to give people information about what was happening in the colonies.

Samuel Adams, Paul Revere and John Hancock helped organise protests and boycotts against Great Britain.

Think about it

Think about the phrase "no taxation without representation". Why do you think this became such a powerful motto?

The Tea Act

Prime Minister North came up with an idea to raise money. In 1773, the British government passed the Tea Act.

By the 1770s, Great Britain had more money problems. The country had a large debt from the Seven Years' War, and the East India Company was also struggling. The company had a **surplus** of tea that it could not sell. This was due to the amount of tea being smuggled into the **market**. It was also making less money than usual in India because of a **drought**. The drought meant there were fewer tea leaves to harvest.

SELLING DIRECT

Before the Tea Act, the East India Company sold their tea to colonial merchants. These traders sold it to American colonists at a slightly higher price. The traders also sold smuggled tea at a lower price. The Tea Act let the East India Company sell tea directly to the **consumer** at a price even cheaper than the smuggled tea, instead of selling it to the merchants first.

The new law meant that the East India Company could offer its tea at a lower price than smuggled tea.

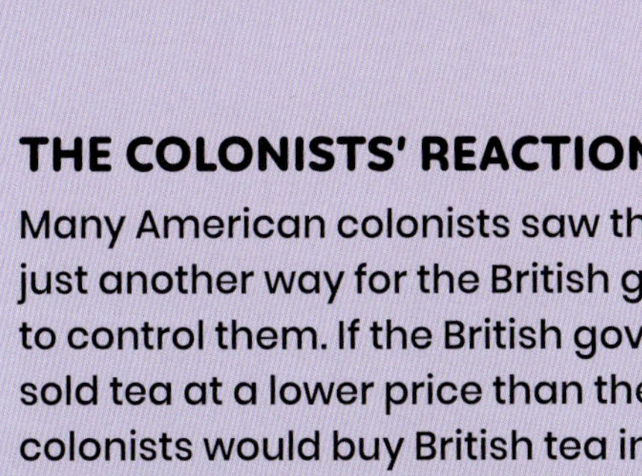

THE COLONISTS' REACTION

Many American colonists saw the Tea Act as just another way for the British government to control them. If the British government sold tea at a lower price than the smugglers, colonists would buy British tea instead of the more expensive smuggled tea. But thanks to the Townshend Acts, the cheaper British tea was highly taxed. So, all the taxes paid by the colonists would go to the British government and they would have full control over the price of tea. Great Britain stood to make lots of money from the colonists.

American colonists were outraged by the Tea Act. The British government was limiting their freedom and making money from them. And worse, they had no say over how they were governed.

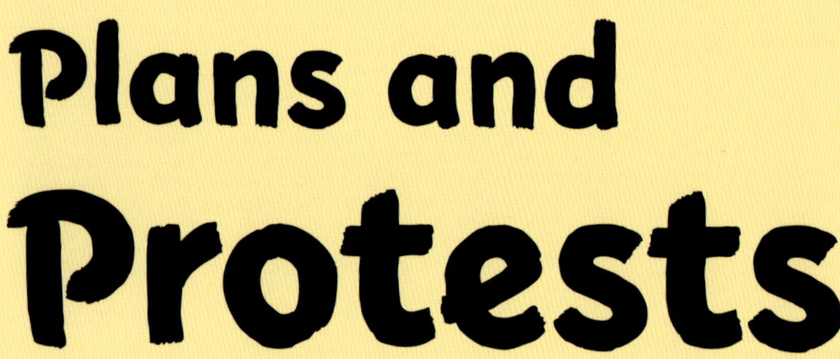

Plans and Protests

The Tea Act increased the existing tensions between American colonists and the British government. Shipments of East India Company tea arrived in the colonies, but the colonists refused to unload any of the cargo.

American colonists saw the tea as a symbol of British **oppression**. They felt that unloading it meant accepting British control over their lives.

In Boston, colonists wanted to send the ships of tea back to Great Britain. But Thomas Hutchinson, the governor of Massachusetts, refused. He insisted that the tea be unloaded, taxed and sent to market.

Fascinating fact

The name "Sons of Liberty" came from a speech by the British politician Isaac Barré. He defended the American colonists and called them the "sons of liberty". This phrase inspired the colonists to **unite** against unfair British taxes and laws.

BOILING POINT

Governor Hutchinson refused to send the East India Company's ships of tea back to Great Britain. This made tensions between American colonists and the British leaders even worse. The colonists had tried protests and boycotts. They had refused to unload the shipments. But nothing had worked. The Sons of Liberty decided to take action.

STRONGER TOGETHER

The Sons of Liberty held public meetings. They explained what the Tea Act meant, and they gathered support against it. Colonists from all walks of life came to the meetings. This included rich merchants, skilled workers and poor labourers. They came together to stand up against unfair British rules. The group's discussions focused on how important it was for everyone to join forces and defend their rights.

The Sons of Liberty had been planning their protest for at least two weeks before the events of 16 December 1773. Late in the day, around 150 members met at Griffin's Wharf in Boston Harbor. They were ready to take action against the Tea Act.

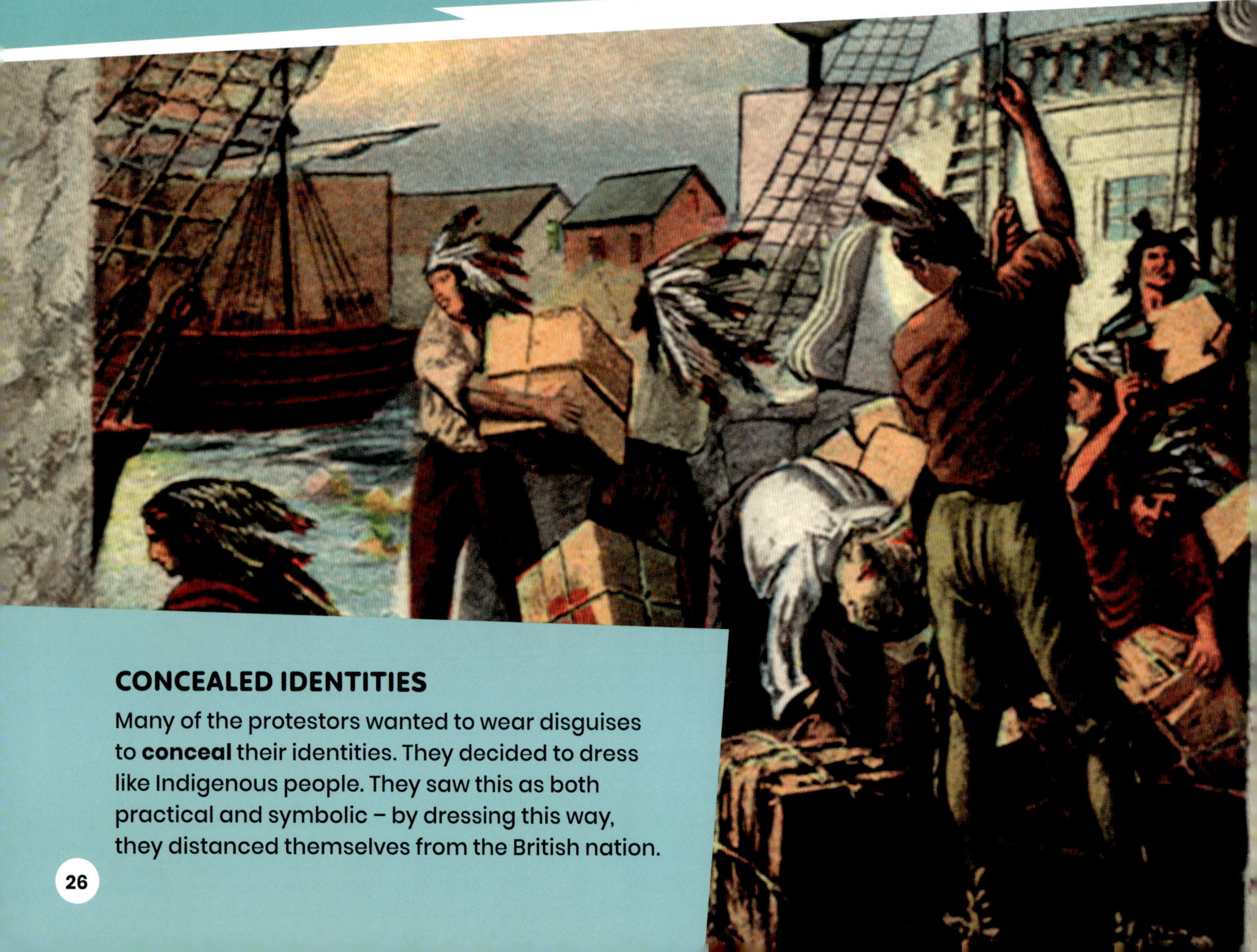

CONCEALED IDENTITIES

Many of the protestors wanted to wear disguises to **conceal** their identities. They decided to dress like Indigenous people. They saw this as both practical and symbolic – by dressing this way, they distanced themselves from the British nation.

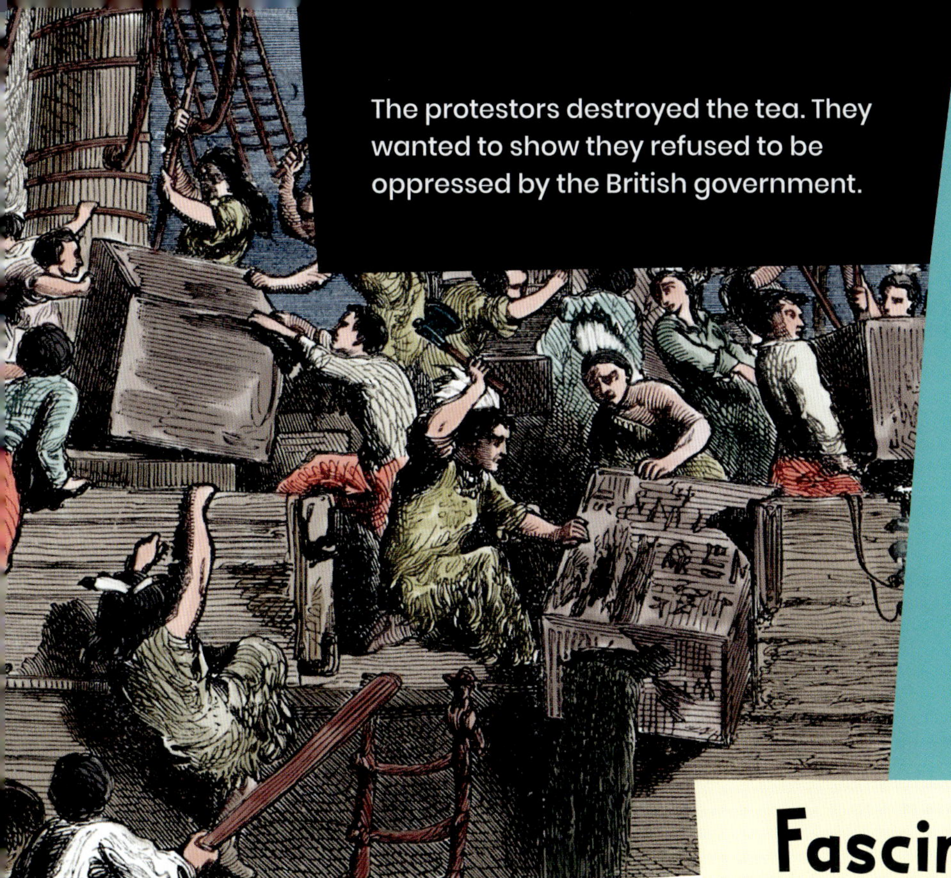

The protestors destroyed the tea. They wanted to show they refused to be oppressed by the British government.

TEA OVERBOARD

The protestors boarded the ships and destroyed 342 chests of tea over a period of about three hours. In total, they dumped an estimated 41,700 kg (about 92,000 lb) of tea into the sea. The tea had cost the East India Company around £9,600 at the time, which is about £1.3 million in today's money.

Fascinating fact

Some of the dumped tea washed up nearby on the shore. There is a small container of tea believed to have come from the Boston Tea Party on display at the Boston Tea Party Ships and Museum.

AUTHORITIES ENRAGED

Many people gathered at the harbour to see what was happening. Some were excited, while others were alarmed and worried about the consequences. They feared the protest could lead to severe punishment from the British authorities. British officials were furious. They viewed the Boston Tea Party as an act of **treason** and a direct challenge to their **authority**.

Trouble Brewing

King George III
King of Great Britain and Ireland, and the head of the British Empire

Lord North
Prime minister of Great Britain

Samuel Adams
A founder and senior member of the Sons of Liberty

John Hancock
A member of the Sons of Liberty

Paul Revere
A member of the Sons of Liberty and a military officer

The Sons of Liberty
An organisation formed in 1765 to oppose British rule and their recently introduced tax policies

May 1773. St James's Palace, London, Great Britain.

Your Majesty, we intend to sell tea directly to the colonies. It will raise money through taxes and save the East India Company from ruin.

Your Majesty, the Tea Act will raise funds and assert our authority over the colonies.

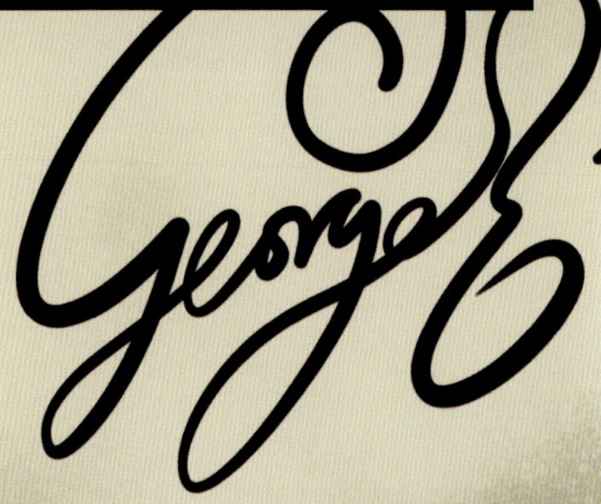

November 1773. A tavern in Boston, America.

Some of the Sons of Liberty met in secret to discuss how to stop the Tea Act.
Governor Hutchinson refuses to send the tea ships back to Britain.

Enough of this! We must STOP the Tea Act!

What if we were to dispose of the tea ourselves?

We will need to wear disguises.
What about wearing Indigenous dress?

I will organise a meeting. This will not fail.

The plan to destroy the tea was underway.

December 1773. The Sons of Liberty met at the Old South Meeting House.
Governor Hutchinson insists we unload the tea and pay the tax.
No!
No!
Hush!
Shhh...
But we have a plan. We are going to seize the tea and destroy it!
Liberty forever!
The British think we will keep paying them taxes but not demand the vote. They are wrong, and this will show them!

January 1774. St James's Palace, London.
Your Majesty, I bring troubling news from Boston.
What is it?
The colonists have destroyed a whole shipment of tea. They threw it into the harbour.
The Sons of Liberty had dumped all 342 chests of tea into Boston Harbor.
This is an act of rebellion! It must not go unpunished!
Your Majesty, we will punish them. Let's close the harbour and ban public meetings.
Map No. 5.
ENGLISH COLON
Yes, make an example of Boston. Show them that the colonies must do as we say.
We have built an empire that is the envy of the world. It will never crumble.

Not Tolerable!

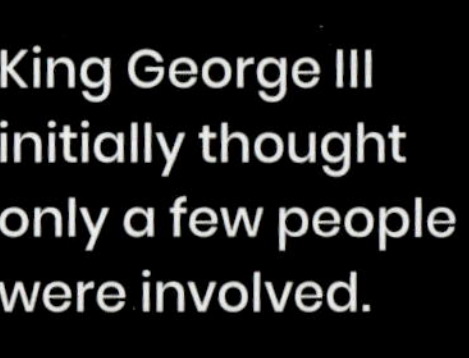

King George III initially thought only a few people were involved.

News of the Boston Tea Party soon reached Great Britain. When he first heard the news, King George III thought it was a minor setback caused by a few **vandals** in Boston. Prime Minister North saw it differently. He was very angry. He insisted that Massachusetts would pay for the destroyed tea.

THE BRITISH REACTION

In response to the events at Boston Harbor, Prime Minister North led the British government to quickly introduce a series of harsh new measures. These became known as the Intolerable Acts. The acts included shutting down Boston Harbor, which stopped almost all trade. This made it very hard for people to work and earn money. The British even sent the Royal Navy to watch over the harbour to ensure it stayed closed.

Prime Minister North supported the new laws that forced American colonists to give British soldiers a place to stay. The laws also stopped local towns from having their own meetings. The American colonists were frustrated, worried and angry. They had fought for freedom but faced even more constraints. There was no doubt – Massachusetts was controlled by the king.

The *Whitehall Pump* is a British cartoon from 1774. It portrays how the British government treated the American colonies after the Boston Tea Party. In it, Prime Minister North is pumping water over people representing Great Britain and the American colonies.

NO WINNERS

The *Whitehall Pump* cartoon shows how the Intolerable Acts hurt both the American colonies and Great Britain. For the colonies, the laws impacted their economy and reduced their freedoms. They made many people angry and united them against Britain. For Britain, enforcing these acts was costly and damaged trade and their control over the colonies.

COLONIST ANGER

American colonists were unhappy that they were not allowed to send the tea back to Britain. They were also furious about the impact of the Intolerable Acts on Boston's people. Pamphlets and newspapers spread anti-British feeling, and there were small protests in the streets. Some colonists started secretly training for military combat.

One of the acts allowed British soldiers to be housed in unoccupied homes. It did not allow them to take over occupied houses but, as this picture shows, people still thought forced takeovers were happening.

The Road to Revolution

The passing of the Intolerable Acts in March 1774 led to the **First Continental Congress.** It was held in Philadelphia from September to October of the same year. Representatives from 12 of the 13 colonies met. Georgia did not send anyone. At the congress, representatives discussed the Intolerable Acts.

At the First Continental Congress, the representatives discussed how to protect their rights and stand up to the British government.

Think about it

Many American colonists supported Great Britain. Why do you think this was?

The 12 representatives created a document called Declarations and Resolves. It listed their complaints against British rule and asked the public to boycott British products.

THE IDEA OF INDEPENDENCE

At first, the representatives met to discuss how to protect their rights. But as time passed, they started to think about gaining **independence** from Great Britain. The country's treatment of Boston angered the colonists and made them worry about what might happen next.

SHOTS ARE FIRED

The British government feared a **rebellion**. So, they decided to take away the colonists' weapons. The colonists felt that this was a step too far. They believed they had the right to defend themselves from **tyranny**.

In April 1775, British troops marched from Boston 32 km (20 miles) west to the town of Concord to seize the colonists' weapons. On the way, they met groups of American colonists, who were trained and ready to fight. Shots were fired. It remains unknown who shot first. This became known as the Battles of Lexington and Concord. The battles marked the start of fighting, and the American Revolution.

Paul Revere and others famously rode through the night from Boston to Lexington on 18 April 1775 to warn American colonists that British troops were coming. This advance warning allowed the colonists to prepare.

Lessons from History

When the colonists dumped the 342 chests of tea into Boston Harbor on 16 December 1773, they helped bring about great changes. These paved the way for the American Revolution and eventually led to American independence. So why do we remember the Boston Tea Party, and what can we learn from it?

ANNO DECIMO QUARTO

Georgii III. Regis.

CAP. XIX.

An Act to diſcontinue, in ſuch Manner, and for ſuch Time as are therein mentioned, the landing and diſcharging, lading or ſhipping, of Goods, Wares, and Merchandiſe, at the Town, and within the Harbour, of *Boſton*, in the Province of *Maſſachuſet's Bay*, in *North America*.

WHEREAS dangerous Commotions and Inſurrections have been fomented and raiſed in the Town of Boſton, in

The Intolerable Acts made American colonists more determined to live free from British rule.

A TURNING POINT

The Boston Tea Party was a response to the policies of Great Britain, and a turning point in the drive towards independence. The Tea Act, Stamp Act and Townshend Acts annoyed many colonists as they felt that Britain was controlling them without giving them anything in return, and renewed frustrations about lack of representation in parliament. Britain's reaction to the Boston Tea Party, including the Intolerable Acts, ended up uniting the colonies even more against British rule. The Boston Tea Party shows that one event can be the turning point for a revolutionary movement that leads to extensive changes.

This event inspired future generations to continue to fight for their freedom. It shaped the identity of what would become the United States.

Think about it

The American colonists destroyed a lot of tea, but left the ships in the harbour undamaged. Why do you think they chose to do this?

THE SPIRIT OF RESISTANCE

The Boston Tea Party demonstrated the ability of ordinary people to act against perceived oppression. The Sons of Liberty showed how organised efforts could send a powerful message. Dumping tea into Boston Harbor showed their determination and inspired the movements that followed. The colonists were willing to risk their safety, and their courage helped others to stand up for their rights. This eventually led to the Declaration of Independence and the American Revolution.

THE IMPACT ON THE EMPIRE

The Boston Tea Party shows how local resistance can cause great **upheaval** in society and have a huge global impact. The destruction of the tea lost the East India Company money and weakened its authority. When Britain punished Boston, it united the colonies and by challenging Britain's power, they showed the world that the British Empire was not as powerful as it seemed.

Uncovering the Truth

Primary Sources

A lot is known about the people and events of the Boston Tea Party. This is because there are so many primary sources still available to historians today. A primary source is a document or object created at the time of a historical event.

Primary sources include

- official documents
- letters
- diaries
- paintings or drawings
- photographs
- sound recordings
- videos

Photo of original source

MES are
adful,
ímal
oleful
ous; and
AR-LESS.

An Emblem of the Effects of the STAMP

O! the fatal Stamp

NUMB. 1195.

day, October 31, 1765.

THE

ENNSYLVANIA JOURNAL;

AND

WEEKLY ADVERTISER.

EXPIRING: In Hopes of a Reſurrection to LIFE again.

I AM ſorry to be obliged to acquaint my Readers, that as The STAMP-ACT, is fear'd to be obligatory upon us after the Firſt of November enſuing, (the fatal To-morrow) the Publiſher of this Paper unable to bear the Burthen, has thought it expedient TO STOP a while, in order to deliberate, whether any Methods can be found to elude the Chains forged for us, and eſcape the inſupportable Slavery, which it is hoped, from the laſt Repreſentations now made againſt that Act, may be effected. Mean while, I muſt earneſtly Requeſt every Individual of my Subſcribers, many of whom have been long behind Hand, that they would immediately Diſcharge their reſpective Arrears, that I may be able, not only to ſupport myſelf during the Interval, but be better prepared to proceed again with this Paper, whenever an opening for that Purpoſe appears, which I hope will be ſoon.

WILLIAM BRADFORD

The front page of the newspaper included a drawing of a skull and crossbones. The phrase "O! The fatal Stamp" was written underneath.

DIFFERENT POINTS OF VIEW

Primary and secondary sources may tell different stories depending on the views of the people who created them. A member of the Sons of Liberty would have a different perspective from an employee of the East India Company. It is important to question sources – doing this helps us to understand them and understand different perspectives better.

TOMBSTONE EDITION

This news story is a primary source. On 31 October 1765, newspaper owner William Bradford published a special copy of the *Pennsylvania Journal* called the "Tombstone Edition". He wrote the article to show how much he disagreed with the Stamp Act.

Original source text

I am sorry to be obliged to acquaint my readers that as the Stamp Act is feared to be obligatory upon us after the first of November ensuing (The Fatal To-Morrow), The publisher of this paper, unable to bear the Burden, has thought it expedient to stop awhile,

> William Bradford is worried about the upcoming Stamp Act, which starts on 1 November. He calls this day "The Fatal To-Morrow" to show how serious he thinks it will be for his business. He explains that he has decided to stop publishing his paper for a while.

in order to deliberate, whether any methods can be found to elude the chains forged for us, and escape the insupportable slavery, which it is hoped, from the last representation now made against that act, may be effected.

> He thinks the Stamp Act will be bad for the colonies and will lead to a loss of freedom.

Mean while I must, earnestly Request every individual of my Subscribers, many of whom have been long behind Hand, that they would immediately discharge their respective Arrears, that I may be able, not only to support myself during the Interval, but be better prepared to proceed again with this Paper whenever an opening for that purpose appears, which I hope will be soon.

> Bradford asks his readers to pay their overdue subscription fees so he can continue his work when possible.

Look at the newspaper, then read the transcribed version of the text and answer the questions below.

Quick questions

- How do we know that the views in the newspaper article are those of William Bradford?
- How does the image at the top right of the newspaper page show us that he did not agree with the Stamp Act?
- When does the article say that the Stamp Act will take effect?

Discussion questions

- Why do you think William Bradford was against the Stamp Act?
- How do you think opinions written about in newspapers may have had an impact on the people who read them?

Uncovering the Truth

Secondary Sources

A secondary source is a document or object created after the event, or by someone who was not directly involved in the event. Secondary sources can explain or interpret primary sources. They help in understanding an event.

Secondary sources include

- news articles
- books
- media documentaries
- encyclopaedias

THE IMPORTANCE OF THE BOSTON TEA PARTY

The Boston Tea Party was an important event in American history that demonstrated the determination of the colonists to stand up to Great Britain. It showed the colonists that they could go against their rulers in London. The events increased support for independence and played a key role in starting the American Revolution in 1775.

This monument is a plaque situated in one of the oldest streets of Boston. It commemorates the *Dartmouth* ship, the first vessel that the Sons of Liberty boarded during the Boston Tea Party.

This statue reminds people what Samuel Adams did. His actions, including his role in organising the Boston Tea Party, helped change the American colonies forever.

MONUMENTS

One way we remember people and events is through monuments. A monument can be a statue, a plaque, a memorial, a park or even a building. Monuments help us to think about our past, celebrate achievements and recognise the sacrifices made by individuals or groups. They are often found in public places so that lots of people can see them and learn more about what happened in the past.

In 1872, the United States Centennial Commission was formed by a group of business leaders. They wanted to honour the 100th anniversary of American independence. In 1873, they asked artist Anne Whitney to design a statue of Samuel Adams as part of the celebrations.

The figure of Samuel Adams is around 2.7 m (9 ft) tall and stands on a pedestal that is 3 m (10 ft) high. It was put up in 1880, over 100 years after the Boston Tea Party and 77 years after Adams' death in 1803. When it was first made, it was placed in Adams Square in Boston. In 1960, it was moved close to Faneuil Hall, near the Government Center.

Look at the plaque and the statue, then read the information about them and answer the questions below.

Quick questions

- Why is the *Dartmouth* being commemorated in the plaque?
- Why do you think the statue is so tall?
- Why was the statue made so long after the Boston Tea Party?

Discussion questions

- Why is it important to honour historical figures like Samuel Adams with statues?
- Why do you think the decision was made to move the statue close to the Government Center in Boston?

- Because it was built near where the plaque is situated and was the first ship boarded during the Boston Tea Party.
- It is so tall to make him seem larger than life, showing how important he was.
- It was made to mark the 100th anniversary of American independence.

Vocabulary Builder
A Night I Will Never Forget

How might an American colonist who was at the Boston Tea Party describe it to a relative? Read this fictional letter to see how an eyewitness might describe the event. Pay attention to key words that describe what the writer saw and how she felt.

17 December 1773

Dear Aunt Mary,

I must tell you about an incredible event that took place here in Boston last night. The weather was freezing, but I didn't even feel the cold. I was too excited by what **unravelled** in front of my very eyes. It was a bold act of **defiance** against British rule.

The Sons of Liberty had been secretly planning something, but I had no idea. They disguised themselves in Indigenous clothes to hide their identities. Then, they boarded three ships in the harbour. They threw hundreds of chests of tea into the icy waters of Boston Harbor – one tea chest after another. The sight was both thrilling and terrifying! The cheers from the crowd were so loud that my ears are still ringing.

It was such a powerful way of showing that we will not tolerate any more of these unfair taxes. The atmosphere was full of excitement and determination. I can't wait for you to hear more about it when we meet again!

With my fondest wishes,

Elizabeth

Imagine you are an American colonist writing a message about what you saw at the Boston Tea Party. Then use the letter on page 42 and the prompts and word bank below to write your own letter.

- **What happened?**
- **Who was there?**
- **How did you feel?**

Protest	activists, commitment, demonstration, defiance, determination, duty, enthusiasm, laws, outcry, rebellion, resistance, taxation, uprising
Colonial life	assembly, colonist, crowd, gathering, mob, pioneer, settler, throng
Harbour	cargo, concealment, costume, dock, port, ships, waterfront

Glossary

Aristocrat Someone who belongs to society's upper classes because of their wealth or family connections.

Authority The power or right to give orders and make decisions.

Boycott The act of not buying or not using something from a company or country to show you disagree with its beliefs, policies or methods. For example, if people do not like how a company treats its workers, they might stop buying its products to force it to change.

Chancellor of the exchequer In Great Britain, the government official who is responsible for managing the country's finances, including taxes and spending.

Coat of arms A shield-shaped symbol that represents a person, family, organisation or place.

Colonist Someone who settles in a new area with the support of their government. The area usually has other people already living there.

Colony An area or region that is governed by another country.

Commodity Something that can be bought or sold.

Conceal To hide something so that others can't see it.

Consumer A person who buys something.

Crown A term used to describe the monarchy of a country, in this case Great Britain.

Debt Money that is owed to someone or something else.

Declaration of Independence The document that marked the independence of the American colonies from Great Britain and the founding of the United States.

Defiance Not obeying someone or something.

Docked When a boat is located in a harbour.

Drought A long period marked by little rainfall, causing crops to die.

Empire A large area of land that is controlled by one country.

First Continental Congress A meeting between representatives of the American colonies.

Government A group of people who have been given the power to make and enforce laws in a specific area. Everyone who lives in the area must obey these laws.

Great Britain A country founded in 1707 consisting of England, Wales and Scotland. In 1801, Great Britain joined Northern Ireland, forming the United Kingdom. Also referred to as Britain.

Imported Something brought into one country from another country. Goods and commodities are often imported.

Independence Being free from control or influence of another or others.

Indigenous Indigenous peoples are groups of people who are the original inhabitants of a region or area. There may be many different groups of Indigenous peoples within a region, each with their own languages and cultures.

Interest Extra money that has to be paid back to the lender when someone returns borrowed money.

Market A place where two or more people can buy and sell goods.

Merchant Someone who buys and sells things as a job. Also known as trader or shopkeeper.

Motto A phrase that conveys a strong message, usually based on a belief or principle.

Oppression The act of treating people unfairly and denying them their rights.

Parliament A place where the government representatives of a country meet to pass laws.

Rebellion The action of a group of people who refuse to obey their government's authority.

Repeal Undoing a law. If a rule is no longer needed or wanted, the government can cancel it so that it does not apply anymore.

Representation Speaking for and making decisions on behalf of others.

Seize To take hold of something suddenly, often using force.

Skyrocketed To have increased very quickly and dramatically.

Smuggler Someone who illegally brings goods into a country without paying taxes on them. They often hide these goods to avoid getting caught.

Source A written document, artefact or building that provides information relating to the past. Sources are also known as evidence.

Surplus A quantity that is more of something than is needed.

Tax Money paid to the government by individuals and businesses. Taxes can be taken from money people earn, or things they buy or own (like food or property).

Trade routes The pathways used by ships to transport goods for trading.

Treason The act of betraying your own country by helping its enemies or by trying to harm it.

Tyranny Government actions that are seen as very unfair or oppressive.

Unite To come together as one.

Unravelled To come undone.

Upheaval A strong and sudden change that causes chaos.

Vandal Someone who deliberately damages property or things that belong to others.

Index

A

Adams, Samuel 8, 21, 28–31, 41

American Revolution 35

Attucks, Crispus 8, 17

Australia 13

B

Battles of Lexington and Concord 35

Boston Harbor 4, 10–11, 32

Boston Massacre 7, 8, 17, 20

boycotts 6, 7, 18, 25, 35

Bradford, William 38–39

British Empire 12–13, 37

C

Colonial America 6–7, 16–17, 20–21

- and the First Continental Congress 34
- and the Intolerable Acts 32–33
- and the Tea Act 22–27

colonies 4, 13

Continental Congress, First 34

D

Dartmouth (ship) 40

Declaration of Independence 8, 37

Declarations and Resolves 35

E

East India Company 5, 15, 22, 24, 26, 37

Elizabeth I, Queen 15

enslavement 13

F

First Continental Congress 34

France, Seven Years' War 13, 19

G

Garway, Thomas 14

George III, King 9, 28–31

Great Britain 6–7, 8, 20

- cost of war 18–19
- Empire 12–13, 37
- Intolerable Acts 7, 32–34, 36
- leaders 9
- reaction to Boston Tea Party 28–33
- Stamp Act 6, 8, 18, 20
- Tea Act 22, 28–29
- Townshend Acts 7, 8, 19

Griffin's Wharf 4

H

Hancock, John 8, 21, 28–31

Hutchinson, Thomas 9, 25

I

independence 35

Indigenous peoples 13

- in Colonial America 17
- and disguises of the protestors 4–5, 26, 29

Intolerable Acts 7, 32–34, 36

M

maps

- Boston Harbor 10–11
- North America 12

monuments 41

N

North America 12

North, Lord Frederick 9, 22, 28–31, 32

"no taxation without representation" 20

O

Old Feather Store 11

Old South Meeting House 30

oppression, British 24, 27, 37

P

Pennsylvania Journal 38

Port of Boston 11

protests 4, 24–7

R

representation in parliament 4, 8, 20

resistance 37

Revere, Paul 8, 28–31, 35

  Sons of Liberty 21

  artist 17

Revolutionary War 17, 34–35, 36, 37

Royal Navy 12–13, 32

S

Seven Years' War 6, 13

  cost of 18–19

smuggling 15, 22, 23

Sons of Liberty 4–5, 7, 8, 21, 25, 28–31

  meeting place 11

  protests 25, 26–27, 37

sources

  primary 38–9

  secondary 40–1

Stamp Act 6, 8, 18, 20

  in the Pennsylvania Journal 38–39

sugar 13

T

taxation 4, 6, 14, 20–21

  Stamp Act 6, 8, 18, 20

  Tea Act 22–25, 28–29, 36

  Townshend Acts 7, 8, 19

tea 4, 14–15

  and the Tea act 22–23

Tea Act 22, 22–5, 28–9, 36

"Tombstone Edition" (*Pennsylvania Journal*) 38

Townshend Acts 7, 8, 19

Townshend, Charles 9, 19

trade 10, 11, 13

  Colonial America 16–17

  tea 14–15

Treaty of Paris 19

W

weapons 35

Whitehall Pump, The 33

Whitney, Anne 41

Acknowledgments

The publisher would like to thank the following for their kind permission to reproduce their photographs:

(Key: a-above; b-below/bottom; c-centre; f-far; l-left; r-right; t-top)

4 Alamy Stock Photo: IanDagnall Computing (b). **4-5 Getty Images**: Edward Gooch Collection (t). **6 Alamy Stock Photo**: Chronicle (c); North Wind Picture Archives (br). **7 Alamy Stock Photo**: AF Fotografie (tr); The Granger Collection (tl, bl). **8 Alamy Stock Photo**: Pictorial Press Ltd (b). **9 Alamy Stock Photo**: Niday Picture Library (br); North Wind Picture Archives (bl). **10-11 Alamy Stock Photo**: Chronicle (bc). **Bridgeman Images**: Granger (t). 11 Alamy Stock Photo: Charles Stirling (Travel) (br). Bridgeman Images: Peter Newark American Pictures (tr). **12 Library of Congress, Washington, D.C.. 13 Alamy Stock Photo**: Lakeview Images (cr); North Wind Picture Archives (t); Colin Waters (b). **14 Alamy Stock Photo**: North Wind Picture Archives (b). **15 Alamy Stock Photo**: Granger Historical Picture Archive (t). **Getty Images**: Print Collector (b). **16 Alamy Stock Photo**: Chronicle (b); North Wind Picture Archives (t). **17 Alamy Stock Photo**: Chronicle (t); Science History Images (cr); Everett Collection Historical (bl). **18 Alamy Stock Photo**: incamerastock (t); North Wind Picture Archives (br). **19 Alamy Stock Photo**: World History Archive (l, r). **20 Alamy Stock Photo:** North Wind Picture Archives (b); Colin Waters (t). **21 Alamy Stock Photo**: GL Archive (bl, br); IanDagnall Computing (t). **22 Alamy Stock Photo**: Chronicle (bl); North Wind Picture Archives (tr). **23 Alamy Stock Photo**: AF Fotografie (t); AF Fotografie (bl). **24 Alamy Stock Photo**: Niday Picture Library. **25 Alamy Stock Photo**: The Granger Collection (t); North Wind Picture Archives (b). **26 Alamy Stock Photo**: Pictures Now (b). **27 Alamy Stock Photo**: incamerastock (b); Lanmas (t). **32 Alamy Stock Photo**: Iconographic Archive (b); Pictorial Press Ltd (t). **33 Alamy Stock Photo**: North Wind Picture Archives (b). **Mary Evans Picture Library**: Historic Royal Palaces (t). **34 Alamy Stock Photo**: World History Archive. **35 Alamy Stock Photo**: Pictorial Press Ltd (b); World History Archive (t). **36 Alamy Stock Photo**: North Wind Picture Archives (t). **Getty Images**: PHAS (b). **37 Getty Images**: Douglas Sacha (t). **38 Alamy Stock Photo:** The Print Collector (b). **40 Alamy Stock Photo**: Cindy Hopkins (b). **41 Alamy Stock Photo**: Prisma Archivo (t). **43 Alamy Stock Photo**: The Protected Art Archive.

Cover images: Front: **Alamy Stock Photo**: AF Fotografie bl, The Granger Collection c, Science History Images t/ background; **Dreamstime.com**: Cirquedesprit br; Back: **Alamy Stock Photo**: Cindy Hopkins cl, North Wind Picture Archives tl, bl.

All the books in the DK Super History series have been reviewed by authenticity readers to ensure the represented cultures and experiences are accurate.

This book uses language as appropriate to modern contexts. Historical terms that are no longer acceptable may be present in original source materials and images. These sources are included to present authentic insights into history.